Autumn Flower

CW00734262

MARK J. WESTON

Flower arrangements by Jane Weston

Photography by Roger Tuff

Main U.K. Distributors: **FOUR SEASONS PUBLICATIONS**
The Stables, Monxton, Nr. Andover, Hants, SP11 8AT

Reproduction by Colourcraftsmen Ltd.,
Chelmsford, Essex
Printed in Great Britain by
Tindal Press, Chelmsford, Essex

SBN 901131 01 6

PREFACE

Arranging flowers is a fascinating pastime. The tremendous variety of different flowers and foliages which can be used, each with its individual subtlety of colour, shape and texture, make every arrangement a unique work of art.

Some people possess an inherent artistic ability. They have an inborn appreciation of line and form together with a well developed sense of colour. Others are not so fortunate and have to learn by experience, by trial and error and by continual application.

Everyone, whether they be talented or otherwise, can learn basic techniques which will always serve them to advantage in the future. It is this elementary aspect of flower arranging which this book will impart.

Autumn is a lovely time of year and the flowers available in flower shops are inexpensive and in wide variety. This book will show you how to "paint" pictures with these flowers and really enjoy every moment.

Flower arranging is an intriguing hobby and I hope you will now find all your leisure time is pleasure time!

MARK J. WESTON

Other titles

Spring Flower Arranging

Summer Flower Arranging

Winter Flower Arranging

Christmas Flower Arranging

Party Flower Arranging

Church Flower Arranging

Dried Flower Arranging

Instruction Books

The Art of Floristry—Wedding Flowers

The Art of Floristry—Funeral Flowers

Educational Books

ELF (3R's Home Course for Pre-School Children)

Design Books

Gift and Sympathy Flowers in Colour

Wedding Flowers in Colour

CONTENTS

"Oasis"

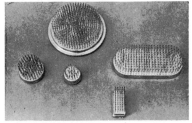
Pinholders

Chicken Wire & Scissors

EQUIPMENT

"Oasis" is a water absorbent plastic foam which is available from your flower shop in several shapes and sizes. Flower stems inserted into "Oasis" are held firmly in position. It should be well soaked in water before use and can be cut with a table knife to the required size. After the flowers have been arranged it is important to keep the "Oasis" continually moist by adding water. When the flowers are finally spent the "Oasis" can be used for subsequent arrangements. There are other plastic foam mounts available such as "Florapak" and "Stemfix" but "Oasis" has been used for all the arrangements in this book.

Pinholders in many shapes and sizes are available from your flower shop. They are a useful substitute for "Oasis" particularly when line arrangements in shallow dishes are required. They can also be used in conjunction with "Oasis" or wire-netting (see below).

Chicken Wire. 2" chicken wire-netting is also an inexpensive flower arranging medium. It should be cut from the roll and crumpled up before insertion into the container.

Scissors. When arranging flowers it is most desirable to use a pair

Compost

of special flower scissors. These have one blade with a serrated edge designed to stop the scissors from slipping on the flower stem. They are readily available from your flower shop.

Compost. When planting bowls it is desirable to use a special potting compost rather than unsatisfactory soil from the garden.

CONTAINERS

The flowers which are to be used together with the particular type of arrangement, govern the choice of the container.

Fourteen different bowls, baskets and dishes are used in this book to portray the seventeen arrangements. All these containers are inexpensive and should be available at your flower shop.

Rectangular Basket with handle. This basket has a metal lining. Filled with "Oasis" it is suitable for triangular and all-the-way round arrangements.

Shallow pottery bowl. With the use of "Oasis" this container is suitable for triangular arrangements. With a pinholder or "Oasis" line arrangements would be practicable.

Oasis Dish. These inexpensive plastic containers are available in two sizes—large and small. Four small spikes are incorporated in the base to take the "Oasis" block. Suitable for most types of arrangement.

Copper Jug. Owing to the curves, this jug is particularly suitable for asymmetrical arrangements.

Rectangular dish. Made of pottery. With "Oasis" or pinholder, excellent for line arrangements.

Pedestal bowl. Made of plastic or pottery. Using a pinholder it is very suitable for line arrangements but is equally suitable for triangular arrangements using "Oasis".

Rectangular basket with handle
Shallow pottery bowl

"Oasis" dish   Copper Jug

Rectangular dish   Pedestal bowl

Round hampers with lid

Square pottery dish   Rectangular basket

Urn   Small plastic bowl

Round Hamper with lid. Basketware. Useful for triangular, crescent or L shaped arrangements.

Square Pottery dish. "Oasis" makes this container very versatile.

Rectangular Basket. Filled with "Oasis" it is suitable for several different types of arrangement.

Urn. Obtainable in white and black. With "Oasis" particularly suitable for triangular arrangements.

Small Plastic bowl. All-the-way round and triangular arrangements look well in this type of container.

Large Plastic bowl. Suitable for planting with flowering and foliage plants. Also could be used for flower arrangements.

Swan. An unusual container. Filled with "Oasis", an asymmetrical curve would complement the line of the swan.

Large plastic bowl   Swan

REMOVING A PLANT FROM ITS POT

1 Holding the pot in the right hand, place the index and middle fingers of the left hand on either side of the base of the plant stem.

2 Turn pot upside-down and gently tap edge of pot against table top to loosen rootball.

3 Remove compact rootball from the pot.

1

2

3

TRIANGULAR ARRANGEMENT

Ingredients
18 stems of michaelmas daisy (2-3 bunches)

8 small sprigs of michaelmas daisy
17 dahlias (2-3 bunches)
2 dahlia buds

1. An ordinary pottery bowl, filled with 'Oasis', is used to take the outline of 9 stems of michaelmas daisy.

2. 9 more stems of michaelmas daisy together with 2 dahlia buds have been added to complete the triangular outline.

3. 7 dahlias have been incorporated and commence the 'filling-in' process which starts at the edges and works inwards.

4. 10 dahlias have completed the arrangement leaving only a few gaps which now require attention.

5. 8 small sprigs of michaelmas daisy have been used to hide the 'Oasis' and add fullness to the final arrangement stage.

Dahlias are justifiably popular with flower arrangers. They come in a comprehensive colour range and several different varieties from the tiny Lilliputs to giant Decoratives. Dahlias are mainly grown outdoors and are fairly weather resistant so availability during their extended growing season is good. They are also inexpensive and, although not very good lasters, represent excellent value. Some of the lily flowered dahlias such as Gerry Hoek and also the 'Twiggy' family are becoming popular because they last well and offer a range of subtle colours. But as usual it is best to follow the advice of your florist.

ALL-THE-WAY-ROUND ARRANGEMENT

Ingredients
40 asters (4-5 bunches)
6 aster buds

1. A basket filled with 'Oasis' has 9 asters and 1 aster bud providing the basic outline and the central aster projects vertically.

2. 9 more asters and one aster bud have been incorporated to complete the horizontal outline.

3. 4 asters together with 4 buds have been used to commence the filling-in from the outer edges.

4. 6 asters continue the filling-in. Note that it is important to graduate so that there is a vertical build up from perimeter to central point.

5. The 12 remaining asters are used to complete the arrangement. There are no residual gaps because asters each have their own substantial 'frill'.

During the Autumn the aster stands out as being of quite remarkable value. All varieties last well as cut flowers and there is a good colour range.

The single as opposed to the double flowered aster are more popular with flower arrangers. The simplicity of shape make them easier to arrange. There is still scope, however, for using the double aster to good advantage.

Make sure that they will take water up their stems when arranged. If the stems are a little on the woody side it is desirable to split up $\frac{1}{2}$'' from the bottom after the usual cutting off of 1'' obliquely with a sharp knife.

CRESCENT ARRANGEMENT

Ingredients
10 sprigs of michaelmas daisy (1 bunch)

16 freesia (2-3 bunches)
7 carnations
9 Kaffir lilies (1-2 bunches)

1. Using a large 'Oasis' plastic dish 8 freesia and 4 Kaffir lilies provide the commencement of the Crescent outline.

2. 2 more freesia and 5 Kaffir lilies complete the outline.

3. 4 carnations have now been added and the filling-in of the arrangement has been started.

4. 3 more carnations have been incorporated adding 'body' to the central part of the arrangement.

5. 6 freesia and 10 springs of michaelmas daisy finalise the arrangement. The michaelmas daisy has mainly been used to fill up any gaps.

When you select carnations from your flower shop, built into the modest cost is the benefit of a vast worldwide research and hybridization programme. Fantastic new techniques are employed which have radically improved the carnation as a cut flower during recent years. Automatically controlled ventilation and irrigation, precise nutrient programmes, the inherent life-time skill of the grower, all combine together to produce this superb cut flower on an all-the-year round basis. Pink, red, white, yellow, orange and mauve are all within the scope of the carnation's colour range and there are a number of 'fancy' varieties as well.

TRIANGULAR ARRANGEMENT

Ingredients
12 chrysanthemum blooms
21 main stems of maple

6 stems of cotoneaster
8 sprigs of maple

1. Using a plastic bowl filled with 'Oasis', 12 stems of maple and 6 stems of cotoneaster foliage provide the basic triangular outline.

2. 9 more stems of maple have been added to complete the outline particularly by projecting over the front of the bowl.

3. 3 chrysanthemum blooms commence the filling-in, starting at the apex of the triangle.

4. 4 more blooms incorporated. Note that no two blooms in juxtaposition are on the same level and all are graduated in height.

5. 5 more chrysanthemums are added to complete the body of the arrangement.

6. 8 sprigs of maple (with autumn colouration) are finally added as gap fillers and 'Oasis' maskers.

ASYMMETRICAL ARRANGEMENT

Ingredients
25 freesia (3-5 bunches)   1 carnation
6 Carole roses   4 rose leaves

1. An elegant china Swan with 'Oasis' is used as the container for this unusual arrangement. 10 freesia stems commence the asymmetrical outline.

2. 10 more freesias finalise the outline, which has tended to follow the contours of the Swan.

3. 6 Carole roses have been used to start the filling-in process. A single carnation inserted close to the oasis provides a centre of interest.

4. 5 freesia have been incorporated and the arrangement is now almost complete.

5. 4 rose leaves have been used to fill up any unfortunate gaps.

For a new rose variety to be a success as a cut flower, stringent requirements are necessary. The rose must be flower productive, disease resistant and compatible with glasshouse environment. It must travel well. It must last well as a cut flower. The colour and shape must be widely acceptable. In spite of these rigid needs it is surprising how many brand new roses are offered each year.

Roses are available from your flower shop throughout the year and are a complete boon to the flower arranger. When autumn comes the prices are still absurdly low so it is worth revelling in their plenty.

ALL-THE-WAY-ROUND ARRANGEMENT

Ingredients
38 anemones (4-5 bunches)
17 sprigs of pittosporum (1 bunch)

1. 13 anemones provide the circular outline. The remaining anemone establishes the overall height of the arrangement.

2. 9 anemones have been used to complete the horizontal outline.

3. 9 more anemones start the essential filling-in procedure working inwards from the perimeter to the centre.

4. 6 more anemones complete the filling-in and the arrangement is nearly completed. A sprig of pittosporum lies nearby awaiting incorporation.

5. 17 sprigs of pittosporum have been inserted at random as gap fillers.

The first flush of anemones comes in the autumn. This little flower lasts extremely well and flower arrangers are quick to take advantage of its charm and beauty.

For some years Devon and Cornwall have been experiencing terrible virus trouble with this flower but with perseverance and extensive research the anemones, coming from these climatically mild districts, are a match for any from overseas. The Channel Islands grow excellent anemones and supply them over an extended season to the Mainland. Availability on a virtual year-round basis is made possible by imports from the South of France, Malta and Israel.

TRIANGULAR ARRANGEMENT

Ingredients
21 freesia (2-4 bunches)
6 gentians (1 bunch)
10 sprigs of pyracantha

1. A square pottery container with 'Oasis' has had 9 sprigs of pyracantha added to provide a partial outline.

2. 7 freesia have been incorporated to complete the triangular outline.

3. 5 more freesia commence the filling-in process.

4. 6 gentians have been used to provide a centre of interest.

5. 9 freesia and 1 sprig of pyracantha complete the filling-in procedure and the arrangement itself.

The containers used for the flower arrangements in this book tend to be basic ones—because the arrangements are basic as well.

In later books in this series more emphasis will be placed upon the container itself as an integral part of a flower arrangement. It is worth looking around for items which may, sooner or later, serve as flower containers. Antique shops, junk shops, china departments can all yield a rich harvest—and it's worth asking your florist what he has "hidden away"! With 'Oasis' and pin holders it is surprising what can be used.

CRESCENT ARRANGEMENT

Ingredients
6 chincherinchees (1 bunch)
6 Roselandia roses
7 yellow carnations
2 stems of spray chrysanthemum
7 rose leaves

1. A small round hamper has been filled with 'Oasis' and 6 chincherinchees inserted to form the commencement of the crescent outline.

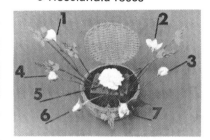

2. 6 yellow roses further identify the outline and 1 carnation marks the centre point of the arrangement.

3. 6 carnations have been incorporated and commence to fill in the outline.

4. 9 individual spray chrysanthemum flowers complete the filling-in and the Crescent is nearly finished.

5. 7 rose leaves fill up any remaining gaps and hide (if necessary) the 'Oasis'.

Autumn is the natural season for chrysanthemums. This is the time they are available from the open ground in a large variety of shapes, sizes and colours. Nowadays chrysanthemums are grown all-the-year round by new specialised techniques, and what a boon this is to flower arrangers. If, after cutting 1'' off the end of the stem and then splitting up another $\frac{1}{2}$'' to 1'', the chrysanthemum flags prematurely, this is a sure sign that water uptake has been blocked. Immerse the last 2'' of the stem in boiling water for two minutes.
This will relieve the blocked capillaries

L-SHAPED ARRANGEMENT

Ingredients
4 yellow gladioli
3 peach gladioli
6 stems of golden rod (1 bunch)
18 stems of dahlia (3 bunches)

1. In a pottery trough 5 stems of golden rod have been used to establish the L shape.

2. 4 yellow and 3 peach gladioli further substantiate the outline.

3. 6 dahlias and one dahlia bud have been incorporated into the L shape. 3 dahlias project horizontally over the front of the container.

4. 11 dahlias, 1 dahlia with buds attached and 2 single dahlia buds have been added and help to fill in the line of the arrangement.

5. 6 sprigs of golden rod have been used as gap fillers and also to add lightness to the completed decoration.

Gladioli, coming from the open, are susceptible to weather damage, but it is surprising how skilful growers manage to keep their flowers blemish free even in adverse seasons.

The giant gladioli is particularly useful for flower arranging because of its 'different' shape and versatile colour range. The miniature varieties are also popular, particularly for the more petite type of arrangement. Gladiolus is a good laster and very accommodating as far as water take-up is concerned. Just cut 1'' off the bottom of the stem before arranging. Remove each floret as it goes over to keep the arrangement neat and tidy.

PLANTED BOWL

Ingredients
1 Cissus antarctica
2 chrysanthemum plants
1 Hedera canariensis
2 Peperomia magnoliaefolia
1 Kalanchoe

1. In a plastic bowl partially filled with special potting compost, one Cissus antarctica, removed from its pot (see page 7), is positioned at the back.

2. Two small chrysanthemum plants, after removal from their pots, are added.

3. A Hedera canariensis is now incorporated to the right-hand side of the bowl.

4. 2 Peperomia magnoliaefolia are added towards the front. The variegated foliage helps to lighten the arrangement.

5. Finally a Kalanchoe is removed from its pot and placed in the remaining frontal gap. The plants are now firmed down into their final locations and the bowl topped up with compost.

Since the war there has been a revolution in the world of indoor foliage plants and a vast range of intriguing common and rare specimens, originating from all parts of the world, are now readily available. They represent extremely good value because they are mostly good lasters. It is best, however, to seek the advice of your florist because some of the most attractive plants are also the most temperamental and delicate Flowering plants are also worthy of consideration for room and office decoration. Regular visits to your flower shop will ensure that you keep up to date with the new arrivals!

TRIANGULAR ARRANGEMENT

Ingredients
12 Carole roses
12 single asters (say 1-2 bunches)

1. Using a round basketware hamper with lid 5 Carole roses have been inserted into 'Oasis' to form the basic triangular outline.

2. 2 **more** Carole roses together with 4 single asters have been incorporated to continue forming and filling-in the outline.

3. 2 roses finally complete the outline. 3 Carole roses have been inserted in the front of the arrangement projecting from 2'' to 3''.

4. 4 single asters and 2 aster buds have been added to the central part of the arrangement and commence the filling-in.

5. 4 more asters complete the arrangement. Aster No. 3 has been deeply recessed to give vertical depth.

There are two essential factors which govern how long cut flowers will last. Firstly water must readily flow up the stem. Soft stemmed flowers such as anemones require 1'' cut off the bottom of the stem before being placed in water (or 'Oasis'). Woody stemmed flowers such as roses in addition to the removal of 1'' of stem after that require the stem splitting or crushing before going into water. The second factor is temperature. The lower this is (down to about 40°F) the longer the flowers will last. So choose a location for your arrangements, out of direct sun and away from radiators.

LINE ARRANGEMENT

Ingredients
9 carnations
5 pieces of rhododendron

1. A shallow pedestal bowl with pinholder is used for this arrangement. 3 carnations establish the vertical height.

2. 3 more carnations complete the vertical line. Note how the carnations are all graduated in length.

3. 1 short carnation has been recessed close to the pinholder. The other 2 carnations are projected 1'' and 3'' over the front of the bowl.

4. 5 pieces of rhododendron foliage have been incorporated to show off the carnations to their best advantage and finalise the arrangement.

Foliage serves two distinct purposes as far as flower arranging is concerned. It can either be used as a complement or a substitute for flowers and be assembled into the arrangement as an outline or in the main body. Alternatively certain foliages lend themselves well as gap-fillers when putting the final touches to the arrangement.

During the autumn the flower arranger is well served with foliages. The berried shrubs such as cotoneaster and pyracantha are available as well as the autumn tinted maples, oaks and beeches. The evergreens such as box, rhododendron, pine and laurels are also on sale. Pittosporum from the West country together with eucalyptus populus and grevillea make their welcome reappearance.

Some people preserve their own beech with glycerine/water solutions with varying degrees of success but your flower shop will probably have some of the super Italian treated foliage which will last until you are sick of it.

In 'Winter Flower Arranging' (one of the companion volumes to this book) you will see an all-foliage arrangement which looks charming and is essentially a practical proposition for an unusual and long-lasting arrangement.

ALL-THE-WAY-ROUND ARRANGEMENT

Ingredients
33 sprigs of heather

1 bunch of outdoor spray chrysanthemum to supply 27 flower heads and buds

1. An 'Oasis' dish has been used and the arrangement outlined with 17 sprigs of heather. 2 chrysanthemum buds establish the approximate height.

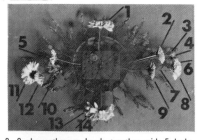

2. 9 chrysanthemum heads together with 5 buds have been incorporated to give further substance to the outline.

3. 7 chrysanthemum heads and 8 chrysanthemum buds have been used to commence filling-in from the perimeter.

4. 11 more chrysanthemum heads complete the build up from the edges to the centre.

5. 16 sprigs of heather fill in any gaps remaining and complete the arrangement.

New and unusual varieties of chrysanthemums are becoming more readily available. The Spiders and Rayonantes particularly lend themselves to flower arranging. Also the single-flowered varieties. All these are grown by specialist growers on an all-the-year round basis not only as spray chrysanthemums but also quite often as individual blooms.

Chrysanthemums are very good lasters but, the environmental temperature is of great importance. It is worth placing arranged containers in a few inches of cold water in the bath overnight. The coolness and humidity will startingly revive even wilted arrangements.

ASYMMETRICAL ARRANGEMENT

Ingredients
1 bunch bronze spray chysanthemum

1 bunch yellow spray chrysanthemum (outdoor)

1. 4 stems of outdoor spray chrysanthemum have been inserted into the 'Oasis' in a copper jug and commence the asymmetrical outline.

2. Another 3 stems of chrysanthemum further substantiate the outline.

3. 3 more stems nearly complete the curving outline.

4. more stem has been used to complete the outlin and another 3 have been incorporated as part of the filling-in process.

5. 6 flower heads are used for filling-in and leave the arrangement nearly complete.

6. Several buds (9) are added to fill up any gaps, mask the 'Oasis' and generally help to lighten the arrangement.

TRIANGULAR ARRANGEMENT

Ingredients
23 dahlias (say 4 bunches)

1. Using a pottery urn filled with 'Oasis' 10 dahlias have been incorporated to form a triangular outline.

2. 2 dahlias have been inserted to project from 4''–5'' over the front of the urn. 3 buds have been added to the outline.

3. 3 dahlias and 4 buds have been used to commence filling-in the arrangement. Note No. 5 has been recessed as a centre of interest.

4. 4 more dahlias and 1 bud further help with the filling-in of the main body of the arrangement.

5. 4 dahlias complete the filling-in process.

6. 5 dahlia buds together with 3 clusters of dahlia leaves have been added to hide any gaps.

L-SHAPED ARRANGEMENT

Ingredients
1 bunch michaelmas daisy
6 chrysanthemum blooms

1 bunch spray chrysanthemum (outdoor)

1. A basket with handle, has had 6 stems of michaelmas daisy and 4 stems of spray chrysanthemums incorporated at the three salient points.

2. 7 stems of spray chrysanthemums have been used to substantiate the vertical line and to project over the front of the container.

3. 7 chrysanthemum spray flower heads together with buds have been incorporated to finalise the L-shaped outline.

4. 3 pink chrysanthemum blooms add body to the arrangement and further substantiate the distinctive outline.

5. 3 more blooms (white) complete the arrangement except for the final gap-filling.

6. 3 sprigs of michaelmas daisy and 4 heads of chrysanthemum spray have been incorporated as stop gaps.

LINE
ARRANGEMENT *(see cover)*

Ingredients
6 chrysanthemum blooms
6 pieces of beech

1 Using a shallow pottery trough and pinholder, 2 chrysanthemum blooms have been used to commence the vertical line.

2. 2 more blooms, graduated in height, complete the vertical aspect of the arrangement.

3. 1 bloom is recessed to give depth to the arrangement, the other bloom projects towards the front and finalises the line.

4. 6 pieces of beech foliage soften the blooms and provide a finishing touch to the arrangement.

Booksellers offer attractive book tokens for any amount which can be sent by post and exchanged at any convenient bookshop. This is a marvellous service and solves many gift problems. Florists also offer a unique gift service. Two world-wide relay services—Interflora and British Teleflower—enable flowers to be sent anywhere in the world for delivery at very short notice. And what more delightful and acceptable present than flowers or plants. So when you start your "Christmas present" list bear these two excellent services in mind and solve your gift problems the easy way!

Incidentally, all florists are experienced at arranging flowers—it is part of their job. So, next time, instead of just asking for flowers to be sent why not instruct for a flower arrangement or planted bowl instead. The busy recipient and the hospital patient (and the nurses) will all thank you even more than usual.

Many people think it is rude not to send "Thank you" flowers to their hostess to show how much the hospitality has been appreciated. This is where Interflora and British Teleflower come into their own once again. It is small gestures like this that are so greatly valued.